ARCTIC OCEAN
SEVERNAYA ZEMLYA
FRANZ JOSEF
NEW SIBERIAN ISLANDS
RUSSIA
FINLAND
ESTONIA
LATVIA
LITHUANIA
BELARUS
UKRAINE
MOLDOVA
ROMANIA
BULGARIA
GREECE
TURKEY
GEORGIA
ARMENIA
AZERBAIJAN
KAZAKHSTAN
UZBEKISTAN
KYRGYSTAN
TURKMENISTAN
TAJIKISTAN
MONGOLIA
CHINA
NORTH KOREA
SOUTH KOREA
JAPAN
NORTH PACIFIC OCEAN
CYPRUS
SYRIA
IRAQ
IRAN
AFGHANISTAN
JORDAN
KUWAIT
PAKISTAN
NEPAL
EGYPT
SAUDI ARABIA
QATAR
UNITED ARAB EMIRATES
OMAN
YEMEN
INDIA
BANGLADESH
MYANMAR (BURMA)
LAOS
THAILAND
CAMBODIA
VIETNAM
PHILIPPINES
GUAM
FEDERATED STATES OF MICRONESIA
MARSHALL ISLANDS
SUDAN
ERITREA
DJIBOUTI
ETHIOPIA
SOMALIA
CENTRAL AFRICAN REPUBLIC
DEM. REP. OF THE CONGO
UGANDA
KENYA
RWANDA
BURUNDI
TANZANIA
SEYCHELLES
ADAMAN ISLANDS (INDIA)
NICOBAR ISLANDS (INDIA)
MALDIVES
SRI LANKA
MALAYSIA
BRUNEI
INDONESIA
PAPUA NEW GUINEA
SOLOMON ISLANDS
KIRIBATI
TUVALU
SAMOA
VANUATU
FIJI
TONGA
NEW CALEDONIA (FRANCE)
ZAMBIA
MALAWI
COMOROS
MOZAMBIQUE
ZIMBABWE
BOTSWANA
MADAGASCAR
MAURITIUS
REUNION
SOUTH AFRICA
SWAZILAND
LESOTHO
INDIAN OCEAN
AUSTRALIA
NEW ZEALAND
PRINCE EDWARD ISLANDS
ILES CROZET (FRANCE)
KERGUELEN ISLAND (FRANCE)

I0869613

GLOBETROTTERS

CAMBODIA

Jane Hinchey

REDBACK publishing

First Published 2023 by Redback Publishing
PO Box 357
Frenchs Forest NSW 2086
Australia

www.redbackpublishing.com
orders@redbackpublishing.com

ISBN 978-1-922322-29-6 HBK

Author: Jane Hinchey
Editor: Caroline Thomas
Design: Redback Publishing
Original illustrations © Redback Publishing 2023
Originated by Redback Publishing

Acknowledgements
Abbreviations: l–left, r–right, b–bottom, t–top, c–centre, m–middle
We would like to thank the following for permission to reproduce photographs:
(Images © shutterstock, wikimediacommons)
p4tr saiko3p, p5 tl Phuong D. Nguyen,p5tr amnat30, p7tr CamNet, p7ml I Love Coffee dot Today, p9tl pablo72, CC BY-SA 2.0 <https://creativecommons.org/licenses/by-sa/2.0>, via Wikimedia Commons, p9mr Adam Jones from Kelowna, BC, Canada, CC BY-SA 2.0 <https://creativecommons.org/licenses/by-sa/2.0>, via Wikimedia Commons, p9bl Pygathrix nigripes, CC BY-SA 4.0 <https://creativecommons.org/licenses/by-sa/4.0>, via Wikimedia Commons, p10tl Christian Inga, p10ml Gaston Piccinetti, p10br Aleksandar Todorovic, p11tr Agent Wolf, p12tr Irina Ovchinnikova, p12mr Mulberry C, p12bl godongphoto, p14br Timgray200, CC BY-SA 3.0 <https://creativecommons.org/licenses/by-sa/3.0>, via Wikimedia Commons, p16tr steve estvanik, p17br Cristina Stoian, p18tl steve estvanik, p18bl https://www.flickr.com/photos/flowcomm/49633491346/in/photostream/, p19tl Emil Litov, p19b Nevskii Dmitrii, p20tl United States. Central Intelligence Agency, Public domain, via Wikimedia Commons, p20br AngkorVector, p22,23m Baldiri, CC BY-SA 3.0 <http://creativecommons.org/licenses/by-sa/3.0/>, via Wikimedia Commons, p23tr Nido Huebl, p24tl Thanachet Maviang, p25bl Gail Palethorpe, p26tr Nido Huebl, p27tl Wirestock Creators, p28tl David Bokuchava, p30t somjai ledlod, p31tl USAID U.S. Agency for International Development, Public domain, via Wikimedia Commons, p31br Stefano Ember

NATIONAL LIBRARY OF AUSTRALIA
A catalogue record for this book is available from the National Library of Australia

CONTENTS

Map of Cambodia 4
Welcome to Cambodia 6
Economy 7
People 8
Daily Life 10
Education 11
Health 12
Sport 13
Religion 14
Traditional Houses 15
Food 16
Transport 17
The Arts 18
The Angkorian Era 20
Angkor Archaeological Park 22
Civil War 24
Geography 26
Climate 28
Flora and Fauna 29
Flags, Symbols and Anthem 30
Glossary and Index 31

MAP OF CAMBODIA

The Royal Palace
PHNOM PENH

Angkor Wat
SIEM REAP

Reclining Buddha
SIHANOUKVILLE

Ta Dambong Square
BATTAMBANG

Salt field
KAMPOT

Floating village
TONLÉ SAP LAKE

SNAPSHOT

COUNTRY
Kingdom of Cambodia

CAPITAL
Phnom Penh

OFFICIAL LANGUAGES
Khmer

AREA
181,035 square kilometres

POPULATION
17,326,923 (2023)

HIGHEST POINT
Phnom Aural, 1,813 metres

RELIGION
Buddhism

CURRENCY
៛ Cambodian Riel

GOVERNMENT
Parliamentary democracy

Did you know?

Cambodia is a constitutional monarchy where the King reigns but does not rule. It is also a parliamentary democracy, and is governed by a Prime Minister who is appointed by the King.

WELCOME TO CAMBODIA

The Mekong River is an essential source or water, income and transportation

The Kingdom of Cambodia is in Southeast Asia, bordered by Laos to the north, Vietnam to the east, Thailand to the west, and the Gulf of Thailand to the south. It is a country with abundant natural resources and a wide variety of fauna and flora. Cambodia is a land of plains and jungles, with important river systems.

The Khmer people are still rebuilding after a civil war. Many people live in poverty, however the country's economy has expanded rapidly in recent years offering more opportunities for many families to live more comfortable lives.

Main Exports:

Exports include garments, petroleum, gold and automobile parts.

Main Imports:

Petroleum products, fabrics, medicine, vehicles, wholesale yarn, cigarettes and electrical communications equipment.

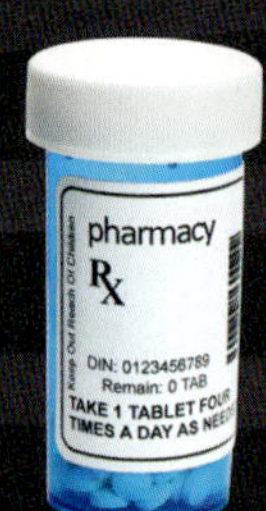

ECONOMY

In recent times, Cambodia has had one of the fastest growing economies in the world and is one of the fastest-growing developing countries in Asia.

Goods are imported and exported through Sihanoukville Autonomous Port

Garment factories employ over 750,000 people - mostly women

Major Industries and Natural Resources

Cambodia's major industries are garments and textiles, light manufacturing such as bicycles, electronics, tourism and agriculture.

The nation's natural resources include gold, copper, bauxite, iron ore, coal, oil and gas.

Home Grown

Cambodia's main agricultural products are rice, sugarcane, corn, coconuts, tobacco, coffee, peanuts, tea and fruits such as bananas, oranges, mangoes and papayas.

PEOPLE

Cambodia has a population of over 17 million people, most of whom are ethnic Khmer. The remaining groups include Chinese-Khmers, Khmer Islam (or Chams), ethnic hill-tribe people (Khmer Loeu) and Vietnamese.

Most of Cambodia's population are Khmer

Khmer

Nine out of every ten Cambodians are Khmer. Traditionally, the Khmer are farmers, but in recent years many have moved to urban areas looking for work. Most live in villages, usually near bodies of water. The Khmer practice Theravada Buddhism and acknowledge the spirits of their ancestors. They speak Khmer.

Vietnamese

There are an estimated 700,000 Vietnamese living in Cambodia. They settled in Cambodia during French colonial rule and many are stateless residents. Most Vietnamese do not hold citizenship papers, birth certificates or identity papers. The Vietnamese mainly live in impoverished communities in rural parts of Cambodia. They practise Mahayana Buddhism, Cao Đài or Catholicism, and speak Khmer and Vietnamese.

Many Vietnamese residents of Cambodia do not own identity documents

Did You Know?

Most Cambodians don't celebrate their birthdays. Many older Cambodians don't even know when they were born.

Chinese New Year celebrations in Phnom Penh

Chinese

Chinese immigrants first arrived in Cambodia in the 3rd century BC. Traditionally they have been merchants and traders, which made them vulnerable during the Khmer Rouge era when business was banned. Today, the Chinese have regained much of their previous economic prosperity. Most Chinese are practitioners of Taoism, Confucianism and Buddhism.

Chams

Chams are Muslim and speak the Cham language. In the countryside, Cham live in their own villages, often directly next to Cambodian villages. In the cities, they live in their own neighbourhoods or suburbs. Many Cham are employed in fishing, small business, and raising and slaughtering of livestock. The women weave silk and mats. Cham women have long hair and cover their heads with scarves while men wear skullcaps and often grow beards.

Cham women cover their long hair with scarves

Khmer Loeu

The Hill Tribes are isolated and can maintain traditional cultural practices

The Khmer Loeu are also collectively known as Hill Tribes because most live in the highland plateaus and valleys. There are around 140,000 Khmer Loeu across many different tribes. They migrated to the region thousands of years ago and are considered indigenous to Cambodia. Because of their geographical isolation they generally avoided becoming victims of the Khmer Rouge and have been able to maintain their cultures and traditions.

DAILY LIFE

Traditionally, family is the basis of the Khmer society. Families are often large and multiple generations frequently live together in one household. Men are head of the household while women control the family budget. Children are expected to respect their elders and later take care of the elderly. Until recently, most Khmer were farmers, however they are increasingly choosing to migrate to urban areas.

Reincarnation

Cambodians generally accept that one's present situation in life is preordained and part of a cycle of many lives, due to the Buddhist belief of reincarnation.

Around age 13, Cambodian boys can be come novice Buddhist monks

EDUCATION

Between 1976 and 1979, Cambodia suffered through an extreme dictatorship that saw education outlawed. The ruler, Pol Pot, destroyed the education system and murdered most of the teachers. Today there is free public education, with six years of primary school (grades 1-6), three years of lower secondary school (grades 7-9), and three years of upper secondary school (grades 10-12). Many Cambodian parents see education as a way out of poverty and place great importance on it. However, there are still many hurdles to overcome when attempting to get children into the classroom, such as a lack of infrastructure and the fact that children are often needed to work on family farms instead of attending school.

Learn the Lingo: the Khmer language

Te
No

Sues'day (informal)
Hello

Lea hery
Goodbye

Somtos
Sorry/excuse me

Ta neak sok sabay teh?
How are you?

Ta neak chhmos ey?
What is your name?

Aw kun
Thank you

HEALTH

Cambodia's health care system has been rebuilt since the civil war and the broader issues involved in maintaining good health, such as sanitation and clean water, are being addressed. One quarter of the total population of Cambodia lacks access to safe water, and nearly half still don't have access to proper sanitation.

In some rural areas, Cambodians access clean water from wells

Chinese medicine and traditional Cambodian practices remain common in Cambodia

The greatest threat to a Cambodian child is malnutrition

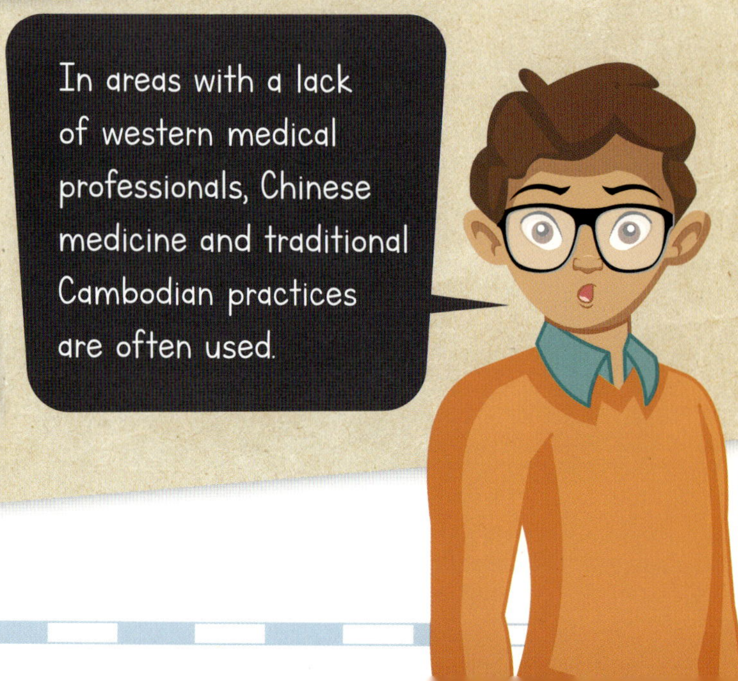

SPORT

Volleyball, soccer, baseball and table tennis are popular sports, as are Khmer kickboxing, boxing and martial arts. Traditional Khmer wrestling has been practised since the Angkorian era, with matches every Khmer New Year and on other important national holidays.

Khmer boxers in action

Sey is a popular Cambodian game in which a shuttlecock is passed around a circle of players

All over Cambodia, every afternoon you'll find young men standing in a circle playing sey, a form of shuttlecock. The aim is to pass the shuttlecock around the circle, keeping it in the air. Traditionally, a sey is made out of four feathers affixed to a rubber sole, but these days plastic is used. The game originated in China more than 2,000 years ago.

RELIGION

A novice monk meditates before a statue of Buddha

The official religion of Cambodia is Theravada Buddhism. Other religions practiced include Christianity, Islam and animistic folk religions. Most Cambodians, no matter what religion, believe in the supernatural world and practice ancestor worship.

The Khmer Rouge period

Buddhism had been the state religion since the 15th century, but during the Khmer Rouge era, all religion was banned and over 50,000 Buddhist monks were killed. After the Khmer Rouge was ousted, Buddhism was revived and temples rebuilt. It became the official religion of Cambodia once again in 1989.

The Buddhist monument at Choeung Ek commemorates victims of the Khmer Rouge

TRADITIONAL HOUSES

Materials

Traditional homes in rural areas have wooden frames, thatched, tiled or iron roofs, walls of timber or woven bamboo, and are raised on stilts to help the flow of air and also protect from flooding. The area under the house is used to relax and keep cool, and to keep animals.

Changing styles

Cambodia has many different styles of traditional housing, depending on wealth, status and region. Traditional wooden homes are being replaced with apartments, shophouses and villas.

Modern style homes are growing more popular throughout Cambodia

Houses are traditionally built to face the east, because Cambodians believe that shows respect to the sun, which in turn brings prosperity to the occupants.

FOOD

Mealtimes

Meals are served on a mat on the floor or with the diners seated together on a raised bamboo platform. Meals are eaten in shifts according to status, with adult males and guests eating first. Fish and rice are staples.

Street food is an essential part of Cambodia's bustling markets

Daily Diet

Breakfast typically consists of rice porridge or rice noodles. Lunch and dinner may be a combination of a spiced broth with fish or meat and vegetables, a dish of fish, fresh vegetables and a fish-based paste, as well as stir-fried vegetables with chopped meat.

Flavours

The most common flavouring of Khmer food is a strong-smelling fermented fish paste called prâhok. Fruit is often given as a gift and considered a mark of abundance when used to create a display. Teuk Tnaot is a liquid tapped from sugar palms. It is drunk at various levels of fermentation, though not usually with food.

TRANSPORT

Traffic can be chaotic in Cambodia, especially in cities. Scooters and motorbikes are the preferred method for shorter distances, while there are numerous bus companies that travel longer distances. The remork-moto (known elsewhere as tuk tuks) is a large trailer hitched to a motorcycle. In urban areas there are cyclos, which use peddle power.

Tuk tuk taxis are a popular mode of transport

Traditional Cambodian long boats transport goods and people

Maritime Methods

Maritime transport has been important to Cambodia for centuries. In some areas the villages were completely dependent on waterways. Boats range in size and are used to transport goods and people along the extensive waterway system including the Mekong and the Tonlé Sap Rivers.

Bamboo Railway

Cambodia's Bamboo Railway is a tourist attraction now, but in the early 1980s, people used these ingenious carriages to carry goods and people safely across the landmine-infested countryside.

The Bamboo Railway is now a tourist attraction

THE ARTS

Cambodia's cultural heritage was almost lost under the Khmer Rouge. Writers, performers and artists were murdered under the regime. Today there are many initiatives underway to recover and revitalise Cambodia's arts.

Robam Nesat is a traditional Cambodian 'fishing dance' that celebrates the bounty of the river

Circus Stories

One group gaining international recognition is the Phare Circus. Phare performers use music, dance, theatre and modern circus arts to tell Cambodian stories.

Phare Circus artists are students and graduates from Phare Ponleu Selpak's vocational training centre in Battambang

Music

Traditional music ensembles included a variety of instruments such as wooden flutes and reed instruments, bowed and plucked lutes, struck zithers, xylophones and metallophones, kong vong gong circles and drums of different sizes.

Dance

Aspara is the female spirit of clouds and water in both Buddhist and Hindu mythology. Inspired by the aspara images on ancient temples, the Khmer traditional dance form, aspara dance, dates back to the 7th century.

THE ANGKORIAN ERA

An Empire Begins

The Khmer have lived in the region now known as Cambodia for at least 2,000 years. By the 7th century there were several kingdoms constantly at war with each other. Jayavarman II led a series of successful military campaigns against these kingdoms that resulted in the founding of one large territorial state. In 802 AD he proclaimed himself to be more than a king and took the title Chakravartin, 'Universal Ruler'. It is this date that is used to signal the start of the Khmer empire..

Golden wall art shows the glory of the Khmer Empire

Khmer's Golden Age

The Angkorian period lasted from the time of Javarman's declaration, to the early 15th century AD. This was the golden age of Khmer civilization.

The Bayon temple sculptures at Angkor Wat

Greatest Achievement

The Khmer's greatest achievement was the city of Angkor. The architecture and sculpture on the temples makes the archaeological park in today's Cambodia one of the world's most incredible ancient sites.

A Miniature Universe

Angkor Wat is a miniature replica of the universe. Carved in stone, it represents an earthly model of the cosmic world.

THE ANGKOR ARCHAEOLOGICAL PARK

The ancient temple complex of Angkor Wat at Siem Reap

The Angkor Archaeological Park is the remains of the capital city of the Khmer Empire. It extends over 400 square kilometres and includes canals, temples, shrines and tombs, hydraulic structures and communication routes. Angkor Wat is just one temple in a complex of more than 1,000. Temples such as Angkor Wat, the Bayon, Preah Khan and Ta Prohm are now considered some of the most stunning ancient wonders of the world.

The Preah Khan temple was a university of medicine and the area around it is still rich in medicinal plants

Neak Poan was thought to be an ancient hospital

Ta Prohm is one of the more famous temples, used in various Hollywood films

CIVIL WAR

The Tuol Sleng Genocide Museum in Phnom Penh chronicles the Cambodian genocide

The Khmer Rouge (Red Khmer) under the leadership of Pol Pot, ruled Cambodia from April 1975 until January 1979. In 1976, the Khmer Rouge established the state of Democratic Kampuchea. During this time, an estimated two million Cambodians died. Artists, teachers and academics, doctors and Buddhist monks were killed. The culture and heart of Cambodia was destroyed.

Harsh Consequences

The Khmer Rouge ran work camps where people were overworked and underfed. Others died unnecessarily from diseases like malaria. Leisure activities were severely restricted and family relationships discouraged. There were many rules and harsh consequences for those who broke them.

The Khmer Rouge government was overthrown in 1979.

Bracelets left in remembrance of the dead at a killing field in Phnom Penh

The Killing Fields

Scattered all over Cambodia are fields that were used as mass graves. These places were known as the killing fields. About one million people died at these sites.

Landmines

Landmines are explosive traps that are buried just below the ground. They detonate when a person or vehicle applies even gentle pressure to the ground above them. Cambodia is one of the most heavily mined countries in the world. Millions of bombs and mines still litter the landscape, undetonated. As much as 35 per cent of land in Cambodia remains unusable, which impacts agriculture, industry, tourism and the daily lives of the Cambodian people.

In areas that are mined, children, farmers and women collecting water all become victims of this weapon of war. These deadly devices have killed hundreds of thousands of children as they were herding animals, planting crops or just playing.

Finding and dismantling landmines is an expensive and difficult process, but the Cambodian government and a number of international organisations are working towards clearing these mines.

Many Cambodians have lost limbs to landmines and many more have lost their lives

Signs still warn of the presence of landmines

GEOGRAPHY

Cambodia is located in the heart of Southeast Asia. Thailand, Laos and Vietnam border it. The landscape comprises tropical rainforest and fertile cultivated land, with lush highlands rising up in both the northeast and southeast. It has a short stretch of coast to the south, with numerous islands offshore. Both the Mekong River and Tonlé Sap lake are central to Cambodia's economic and cultural life.

Rice farming is a common occupation in Cambodia

Sihanoukville's many beaches make it a popular tourist destination

Fast Facts

Land Area: **181,035 square kilometres**

Coastline: **443 kilometres**

Highest Point: **Phnom Aural, 1,813 metres**

Lowest Point: **Gulf of Thailand, sea level**

Longest River: **Mekong River, 4,900 kilometres**

Largest Lake: **Tonlé Sap, 2,700 square kilometres**

During the wet season, the Tonlé Sap Lake floods, causing the Tonlé Sap River to reverse its flow

Waterways

The dominant features of the Cambodian landscape are Tonlé Sap (Great Lake), the Bassac River Systems and the Mekong River, which crosses the country from North to South..

The Mekong River originates in China, and flows through Myanmar, Laos and Thailand before entering Cambodia. It is the engine of Cambodia's central feature, the Tonlé Sap. The Tonlé Sap Lake (and river) supports an extraordinarily rich and diverse ecosystem.

Monsoon floods make the Tonlé Sap one of the most productive ecosystems in the world

CLIMATE

Cambodians must live with weather extremes

Cambodia's tropical climate is characterised by high temperatures and humidity throughout the year. April and May feature the hottest temperatures while the weather in June sees the monsoon pattern bringing heavy rain through to October. The climate varies by region, with cooler temperatures in the mountains to the north.

Nature provides shelter from monsoonal rain

Stormwater from highland areas can damage low-lying homes and businesses

Natural Disasters

The country's location and geography makes it vulnerable to natural disasters such as cyclones and other extreme weather events.

FLORA AND FAUNA

Macaques are common in Cambodia, as are gibbons and langurs

Fabulous Fauna

Cambodia is well known for its rich variety of flora and fauna. The Tonlé Sap Lake is home to more than 100 varieties of waterbirds including several threatened and endangered species. Over 200 species of fish, as well as crocodiles, turtles, macaques, otters and other wildlife inhabit the inundated mangrove forests.

Siamese crocodiles are native to Cambodia and surrounding countries

The Hainan blue flycatcher is found throughout South East Asia

Did You Know

Cambodia was the first country in Southeast Asia to establish protected areas of forest, starting with the forests around Angkor.

FLAG, SYMBOLS AND ANTHEM

A student waves the Cambodian flag in the city of Siem Reap

Flag of Cambodia

The flag of Cambodia consists of three horizontal stripes with an image of Angkor Wat in the centre. The top and bottom stripes are blue while the larger centre stripe is red. Red and blue are the traditional colours of Cambodia. The Cambodian flag was officially adopted on June 29, 1993.

Fast Fact

Cambodia's flag is the only one in the world to feature a building, Angkor Wat.

National Bird

The Giant Ibis is a rare and critically endangered animal. The bird in the photo above has been nursed back to health by the local community.

National Flower

Romduol (*Mitrella mesnyi*)

National Symbol

Angkor Wat

National Anthem

Nokor Reach is the National Anthem. It is based on a Cambodian folk tune.

GLOSSARY

Buddhism religion based on the teachings of Buddha

civil war war between citizens of the same country

cultivated land land that is worked by ploughing, sowing and raising crops

culture practices, beliefs and customs of a society or people

endangered when a species is at risk

genocide crime of intentionally destroying a national, ethnic, racial, or religious group, by killing people

highlands a mountainous or elevated region

hydraulic use of water (or other liquid) pressure to operate a device

independence when a country is ruled by its own people

indigenous first peoples of a country

landmines explosive traps that detonate when they come into contact with a person or vehicle

Mekong River a trans-boundary river in Southeast Asia

monsoon a season of heavy rain

prosperity state of being successful and having a lot of money

reincarnation belief that a dead person's spirit returns to life in another body

sanitation systems for taking dirty water from buildings, to protect people's health

tropical hot, humid climate

INDEX

Angkor 4, 10, 21-23, 29-31
boats 17, 26-27
Buddhism 8-9, 14, 32
Mekong 17, 26-27, 32
Tonlé Sap 4-5, 17, 26-27,
Khmer 6, 8-9, 10-11, 13, 14, 16, 18-20, 22, 24
Khmer Rouge 9, 14, 18, 24
Chinese 8-9, 12
Vietnamese 8
hill tribes 8-9
Pol Pot 11, 24
medicine 6, 12, 23
landmines 25, 32
temples 4, 10, 21-23, 30-31
dance 18-19
The Killing Fields 25
macaques 29
monsoon 28, 32

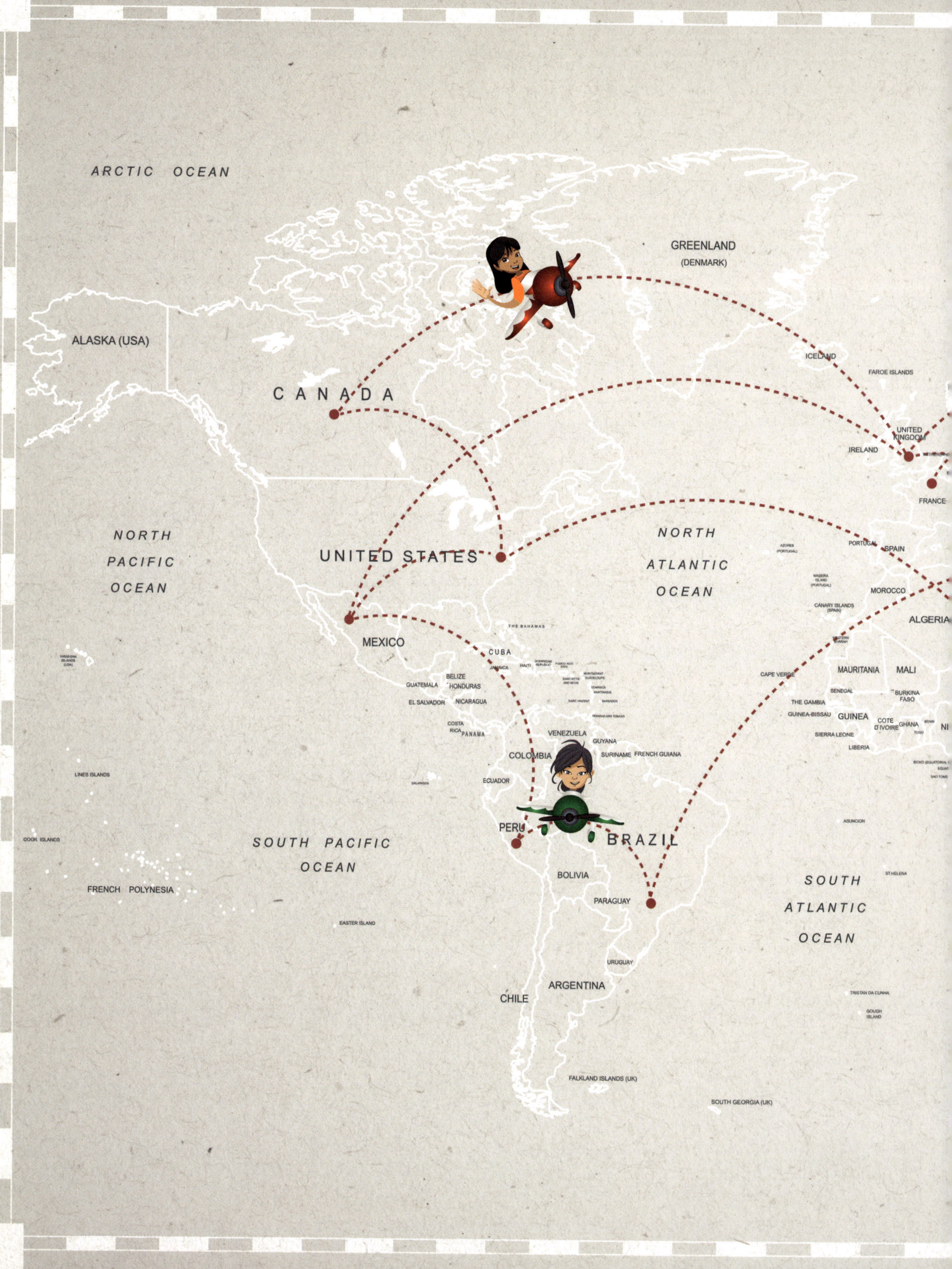
ARCTIC OCEAN
GREENLAND
(DENMARK)
ALASKA (USA)
CANADA
ICELAND
FAROE ISLANDS
UNITED KINGDOM
IRELAND
FRANCE
NORTH PACIFIC OCEAN
UNITED STATES
NORTH ATLANTIC OCEAN
PORTUGAL
SPAIN
MOROCCO
ALGERIA
MEXICO
THE BAHAMAS
CUBA
JAMAICA
HAITI
CAPE VERDE
MAURITANIA
MALI
GUATEMALA
BELIZE
HONDURAS
EL SALVADOR
NICARAGUA
SENEGAL
THE GAMBIA
GUINEA-BISSAU
GUINEA
SIERRA LEONE
LIBERIA
COTE D'IVOIRE
GHANA
BURKINA FASO
COSTA RICA
PANAMA
VENEZUELA
GUYANA
SURINAME
FRENCH GUIANA
COLOMBIA
ECUADOR
LINES ISLANDS
COOK ISLANDS
PERU
BRAZIL
SOUTH PACIFIC OCEAN
BOLIVIA
PARAGUAY
FRENCH POLYNESIA
EASTER ISLAND
SOUTH ATLANTIC OCEAN
URUGUAY
ARGENTINA
CHILE
FALKLAND ISLANDS (UK)
SOUTH GEORGIA (UK)